THE UNVARNISHED TRUTH

A Comedy

ROYCE RYTON

GW00775661

SAMUEL  FRENCH

LONDON

NEW YORK TORONTO SYDNEY HOLLYWOOD

© 1978 BY LUNAGRADE LTD

ISBN 0 573 11465 X

THE UNVARNISHED TRUTH

First presented by the Cambridge Theatre Company at the Civic Theatre, Darlington, on the 31st January 1978: transferred to the Phoenix Theatre, London, on the 13th April 1978, with the following cast of characters:

CHARACTERS

Tom Bryce	Tim Brooke-Taylor
Annabel Bryce	Jo Kendall
Bert Hopkins	Graeme Garden
Mrs Cartwright	Gabrielle Hamilton
Bill Carlisle	Royce Ryton
Mrs Stewart-Dubonnet	Gwyneth Owen
Inspector	Ivor Roberts
Isabel	Morar Kennedy
Dr Sarah Hedley	Joyce Donaldson

The play directed by Jonathan Lynn
Setting by Robin Archer

The action takes place in the living-room of a cottage in Thames Ditton

ACT I Early evening
ACT II Later the same evening

Time—the present

ACT I

SCENE 1

The living-room of a modern cottage in Thames Ditton. Early evening

Leading into the room are the front door, a door to the kitchen, a door to the lavatory, and a flight of stairs with a door and an archway off. Furniture includes a sofa, a day bed, chairs, a desk, two bookcases, a pouffe and a trolley

As the CURTAIN *rises Tom and Annabel Bryce are discovered, a middle-aged couple, kissing each other with great enthusiasm on the sofa*

Tom I love you.
Annabel I love you too.
Tom I love you more than you love me.

They kiss again

Annabel That isn't true, but never mind.
Tom What isn't true?
Annabel What you just said.
Tom About my loving you more than you love me?
Annabel That's right.
Tom You're heaven. (*He kisses her again*)
Annabel You're divine.
Tom Drink?
Annabel Yes please.

Tom gets up, goes to the drinks trolley and pours two drinks

Tom How long have we been married?
Annabel Thirteen years.
Tom Quite a good innings really. Especially as I'm your second.
Annabel You know, I can't remember Paul at all. I can't believe I ever even knew him, let alone married him.
Tom It broke my heart when you did. I remember I went into a decline.
Annabel Well, you soon recovered. You got engaged to Cynthia.
Tom She became a lesbian.
Annabel Didn't your other fiancée become a nun?
Tom Nancy? I believe she did.
Annabel Very sinister.
Tom I shouldn't let it worry you. You actually married me and became neither. Still, it proves my point.
Annabel What point?

Tom You married someone else, whilst I only became engaged to other women. I must love you more than you love me.

Annabel I don't see that it proves anything at all.

Tom You knew I adored you.

Annabel I knew nothing of the sort.

Tom I was in hospital, very ill indeed, and you came and told me you were marrying Paul. The shock was terrible. I had a serious relapse and very nearly died. I had to have four doctors in constant attendance for a week.

Annabel You are funny, darling. None of this is true. I wrote to you about Paul.

Tom I believe you did. All I can remember is the blinding shock. I'd forgotten you didn't have the courage to tell me to my face.

Annabel I wrote to all my friends.

Tom It's a wonder it didn't kill me.

Annabel Darling. You really must be careful. You'll end up believing all this nonsense. We didn't fall in love until after I'd left Paul. We'd lost touch. We met by accident. We went out together and it was then it all started and you know that.

Tom I've decided to forgive you.

Tom sits beside Annabel on the sofa and gives her her drink. She nobly controls her irritation at his words

Shall we go to bed?

Annabel What, now?

Tom It's legal.

Annabel It's legal to drive a car, but I don't see any reason for doing so at the moment.

Tom Oh. Well, that puts me in my place. Thank you very much.

Annabel Darling, I am sorry. I just don't feel like it.

Tom You did a moment ago.

Annabel Yes, I know, but . . .

Tom Come on.

Annabel It would be fun.

Tom Well, then . . .

Annabel Ma's coming.

Tom She won't be here for ages.

Annabel Don't you believe it.

Tom (*rising*) Take that drink, go upstairs and . . .

Annabel There's the supper to cook.

Tom Never mind the supper.

Annabel I must do one or two things first.

Tom God, you are tiresome! We can open a tin. Here I am, full of love for you, full of desire—proper legal desire for my lawful wife—and all you can talk about is cooking supper.

Annabel Well, it's very inconvenient.

Tom Inconvenient! You have no romance in you. The divorce courts are full of women like you, who think more about cooking than they do about the pleasures of the marriage bed. If I had a secretary, I'd ring

her up at once and go out with her. It's quite obvious I love you far
more than you love me. If you'd suggested going to bed, I'd be there
undressed by now, not talking about supper.

Annabel (*rising*) You don't have to cook it. I do.

Tom No, you don't. We could go out.

Annabel Where?

Tom There are hundreds of places in Kingston.

Annabel Mother is very nearly eighty. We haven't booked a table.

Tom I could ring up ...

Annabel You just have no consideration for anyone except yourself and
never have had. Whenever you can't get your own way all the time, you
fly into a rage.

Tom Women are all the same. Practical bitches.

Annabel We have common sense if that's what you mean.

Tom Common sense may be a virtue. I'm sure it is. It's also bloody dull.

There is a pause

Annabel I'm going into the kitchen. (*She turns away*)

Tom Good. When you next appear, make sure you have an overall on,
then we'll all know you're a *hausfrau*. I should also disarrange your
hair and look harassed and overworked and as unattractive as possible.

Annabel You have a very childish streak, darling, but I intend to ignore it.
Will you come and lay the table?

Tom What are we having?

Annabel Soup first, and then—

Tom Oh God!

Annabel What's the matter?

Tom Do we have to have soup?

Annabel No, we don't have to have soup.

Tom Your mother sucks in her soup.

Annabel All old people do. Besides I've made it.

Tom If you've made it already, why can't we go to bed?

Annabel There are other things to do.

Tom There can be no two opinions about it. I love you more than you
love me.

Annabel Oh God!

Tom I don't lie to get out of going to bed with you.

Annabel I haven't lied. I have other things to do. There are the potatoes.

Tom Fattening.

Annabel For her, not us.

Tom You think more about your mother than you do me. What further
proof do you want? Obviously I love you more ...

Annabel (*putting her glass on the trolley*) I'm going to scream. That's what
I shall do. Scream. I shall scream without ceasing all evening.

Tom Well, it's true.

Annabel It isn't. We love each other equally.

Tom You married someone else. (*He sits at the desk*)

Annabel I divorced him, didn't I? In any case, you intended to marry other people. Twice too. I have been loyal and devoted to you for thirteen years. I had faith in your play writing when no-one else had. I've adored you and still do. What more do you want?

Tom I don't doubt any of that. It's just that it's so silly of you not to admit I love you more.

Annabel It's always the same when we get into an argument. You nag round one idiotic point. An idea suggests itself to you and within seconds you believe it.

Tom It's so silly to go on like this when you're in the wrong.

Annabel You can't tell fact from fiction, you never can.

Tom I can.

Annabel You can't.

Tom I can.

Annabel You can't.

Tom I can.

Annabel Darling, do let's stop. It's too silly.

Tom I'm extremely angry.

Annabel Oh dear. I was trying to make it up.

Tom Very successfully too. You should become a novelist. (*Rising*) Your flights of fancy should have a wider public than just me. You may wish to distort the past out of shame at your monstrous treatment of me, but—

Annabel Shame?

Tom (*moving towards her*) Monstrous treatment of me as I lay dying, but I am not going to perjure my immortal soul simply to suit your guilty conscience. (*He moves away*)

Annabel This is too much.

Tom The facts are indisputable. We met as students. We fell in love.

Annabel No.

Tom Then I became ill and you married someone else.

Annabel No, no.

Tom Your first marriage broke up—understandably if you behaved like this—we met again and married.

Annabel Only the last five words are accurate.

Tom Having loved you longer, I loved you more. That alone proves my point. If we consider the question of ardour, only a moment ago I wanted to make love to you and all you could talk about was cooking supper. Obviously, therefore, from every point of view, I am quite right, with a flawless memory of the past, and you are quite wrong. *Voilà!*

Annabel loses her temper, rushes at him screaming and slaps his face

Annabel I love you as much as you love me. (*Slap*)

Tom Annabel darling!

Annabel I love you, I love you, I love you. (*Slap*)

Tom Don't keep on slapping me. It's indicative of hate, not love.

Annabel You're driving me mad. (*Slap*)

Tom Stop slapping me.

Annabel (*kicking him*) I love you, I love you.

Tom Shut up. You've gone mad. I was being sweetly reasonable.

She punches him

Control yourself. ~~Perhaps it's the change?~~ I love you, too. More than you.

She kicks him

Don't kick me like that.

She kicks him

Ow! God, you vicious little slut, no wonder Paul left you. He warned me. He said, "Her temper!"

She punches him

Don't do that. Control yourself. (*He starts shouting*) I love you. Do you hear? *Much, much* more than you love me. I love you. (*He starts to shake her furiously*) You nasty bad-tempered bitch, I love you. I love you.

By this time they are struggling round the room, knocking things over. They fall, and the trolley crashes to the ground. They run struggling, until they are near the standard lamp. She hides behind it, it falls to the floor. They fall on to the bean-bag and struggle on the floor below the sofa. He hurls the bean-bag on top of her. She ceases to struggle. He wanders to the desk

Oh dear. That was terrible. *How* idiotic we are. Who could believe that two rational people with the vote could behave like this? (*He sits at the desk*) I am sorry, truly I am. You did go for me somewhat violently, but I really shouldn't have shaken you like that. You're quite right—about everything. I was maddening.

Annabel lies there silent

Darling? Are you all right? Don't pretend if you are, because you're frightening me. Darling? My God, I've knocked her out! (*He kneels by her, pulls her into a sitting position and slaps her face gently*) Darling. Darling. (*He holds her to him, rocking her gently*) Come on, darling. Wake up. It was such a silly fight. (*Suddenly he stops rocking her and holds her still. He puts her back on the ground and, hardly daring to breathe, holds her pulse*) Jesus Christ! (*His hands go to her heart. He stares at her, horrified*) I didn't mean to do it. You know I didn't. What shall I do? What will become of me? I can't live without you. Oh, please God, let me die now. This minute. I shall kill myself, that's what I shall do. But how? (*He rises*) Gas. It's quite simple. I shall gas myself and they'll think it's a suicide pact. (*He rushes into the kitchen and returns*) Oh dear. We only have electricity. I wouldn't know how to electrocute myself. Aspirins! Obvious. I'll swallow all the aspirins we have. (*He rushes upstairs and reappears holding a large aspirin bottle*) Only three aspirins. That's no good. I'll drown myself. I'll throw myself into the Thames. Or drive off Beachy Head. Or—I'm getting into a panic. It was an accident. If I count ten, I'll feel calmer. One, two, three—I don't feel any calmer—four, five. This won't work. I don't know what to do. Oh, I know. (*He rushes downstairs to the telephone*) Why didn't I think of it before? I'll ring up my agent. (*He sits on the bed and dials a number feverishly*) Hullo. . . . Pamela. . . . Is Bill there? . . . What? . . . Yes, I know it's late. Just put me through to Bill. . . . Out where? He's my sole agent, why the hell aren't I his sole client? . . . He's no business looking after anyone else. . . . No, I'm not all right at all. I'm in a dreadful state. . . . No, I can't explain. . . . Tell him to ring me at once, or better still, come and see me. . . . I don't care if it's midnight. Yes yes. At once. (*He rings off*) How dare he be out when I need him? I shall change my agent. Now, I'm writing a thriller. The hero, an innocent man, accidentally kills his wife. What should he do? He rings his doctor. What's his number? Where's the flap? I can't find it. I can't find it. Ah! Here we are, nine-seven-nine, eight-oh-two-oh. (*He dials feverishly and waits frantically*) AH! I've killed my wife, please come round at once. . . . What's that? . . . What? . . . I've killed my wife I tell you. . . . What? . . . The man's mad. He's not listening to me. . . . This is not a recorded message at all. It's an emergency. . . . Oh. Recorded message. In an emergency ring Dr Headley, nine-seven-nine not so fast! eight-nine-three-oh. (*He rings off and dials again*) Hallo. Can I speak to Dr Headley? . . . You're Dr Headley, I thought you were his wife. . . . Oh, I see, you're him or rather her. . . . Yes, my name is Tom Bryce and I've. . . . My name is Tom Bryce. Bryce. Bryce. B-R-Y-C-E. . . . The idiot's deaf. . . . Oh I'm terribly sorry I didn't realize you were old. . . . I want a doctor. DOCTOR! My wife's dead. . . . No, I realize you're not his wife you're the doctor. . . . My wife's dead. This is an emergency. . . . No, she's not very ill at all. . . . No, it's not all right at all. She's dead. I live at Cosy Nook. COSY NOOK! C for silly cow. O for obstinate and S for stupid. No, I wasn't talking about you. Someone has just come in. Cosy Nook, Ember Way. Hallo. . . . Hallo. . . . Hallo! . . . We've been cut off. Oh God. . . . (*He hangs up and dials again*) No dialling tone. HULLO! (*He shakes the telephone furiously*) Hallo. (*He slams back the receiver*) Please God make this telephone work for once in its life. This one here. (*He picks up the receiver again*) Thank you. Now what do I do? The police. I'll ring the police. I'll explain what happened. I'll be charged with manslaughter. There'll be a trial. I'll get a year or two. And then what? Life without Annabel. I can't face life without Annabel. I couldn't before. I can't now. The police. (*He picks up the local telephone directory*) P. L,M,N,O,P,Q. After O. Before Q. Police. Why can't they write it on the front where you can find it. Here we are. (*He dials a number*) Hullo. . . . Oh, yes. There's been some trouble. . . . Bryce. B-R-Y-C-E. Thomas. . . . I'm a playwright. . . . The Cosy Nook. . . . COSY NOOK! Dreadful name. It's rented furnished. . . . Thames Ditton. . . . I don't feel very well. You see—well, it sounds idiotic, but I love my wife, truly I do. . . . You love yours, too. Oh, I am glad. . . . Well, yes, there's been trouble, and you see—I don't know what to do. (*He hangs up*) I don't know what to do. I don't know what to do. (*He goes to Annabel*) Oh darling, I don't know what to do.

The lights fade to a Black-out

Scene 2

The same. A few minutes later

Tom is sitting by his wife, holding her hand. There is a ring at the front door

Tom Who is it?
Bert (*Off*) Police.
Tom Oh yes.

Tom gets up and crosses slowly to the front door. The body cannot be seen from it

Good heavens!

Bert Hopkins comes in. Slightly older than Tom, he is a policeman, at the moment in plain clothes

Bert Thought it must be you.
Tom Bert.
Bert Constable on duty said you said you were a writer. Well, I thought, there can't be two of you.
Tom What are you doing here?
Bert I'm a copper now. Been one for some time.
Tom Good God!
Bert Doing O.K. now, aren't you?
Tom Yes.
Bert Read about it. I'm so pleased for you.
Tom Thank you.
Bert I often wondered what happened to you. Looked for your name in the *TV Times*. Ever do any TV? (*He steps forward*)
Tom No. (*He blocks his view of Annabel*)
Bert But you get offers now?
Tom Not so you'd notice. I'm afraid I'm totally bewildered. I expected an anonymous policeman. Not someone I knew.
Bert Anyway I am glad to see you again.
Tom Oh, so am I. (*They shake hands*) We must keep in touch.
Bert Sure. What's the trouble? (*He steps into the room*)
Tom (*continuing to block Bert's view of Annabel*) Well, you see . . .
Bert (*seeing the upturned trolley*) Been a burglary? Room's in a bit of a mess. Did you surprise him?
Tom No, no.
Bert Bit of a shock, isn't it?
Tom Yes.
Bert Take your time. I'm in no hurry. I often worried about you. How you got on in civvy street. You were never very practical. Thinking of your plots, I daresay.
Tom I never really quite understood the army. I'd never have survived without you.
Bert What's your play about?
Tom (*after a pause*) Murder.

Bert Well, I hope the police come out of it all right.

Tom Hardly. They plan the crime, execute it, investigate it, falsely incriminate the wrong person, arrest him and he's convicted on their false testimony. They never get caught, but the curtain comes down on them planning a brutal take-over of Parliament.

Bert Crikey! Whatever gave you that idea?

Tom A policeman telling me I'd parked in the wrong place.

Bert It goes to show. (*He now sees the body*) Christ!

Tom That's my wife. She's dead. I'm afraid I killed her.

Bert moves to Annabel's body—feels her pulse and looks at her eyes

Bert Why? (*He rises*)

Tom I didn't do it on purpose. We had a fight. We both lost our tempers and, well, somehow or other we found ourselves rolling all over the floor, and she died.

Bert Did you often fight?

Tom Of course not.

Bert What was the fight about?

Tom (*eventually*) About who loved whom the most.

There is a pause

Bert Tom, you'll have to do better than that.

Tom It's true. I know it sounds idiotic. In fact it is idiotic. I should be certified. So should she, of course. She can't be, I know, but I do hope the Recording Angel has got the facts right. It was entirely her fault. I said I loved her more than she loved me. She argued with me. When she lost the argument, she became quite unreasonable. Declaring with every blow that she loved me, she slapped my face repeatedly.

Bert Repeatedly.

Tom That's right. It's a wonder my face isn't raw and bleeding. It's even more amazing that I'm still conscious. I strove to defend myself from her savage assault. I held her and shook her, we struggled together and tripped and she must have banged her head and killed herself. Now I come to think of it, it was a self-inflicted injury, so in a way I had nothing to do with it.

Bert And then you called the police.

Tom Yes.

Bert Have you touched anything?

Tom No.

Bert Moved your wife?

Tom Of course not.

Bert She's lying where she fell?

Tom I think so.

Bert Think so?

Tom I thought she was just knocked out at first, so I lifted her head and tried to bring her round.

Bert But you didn't actually move the whole body?

Tom No, no.

Bert Well, that's one good thing. (*He shuts the front door*) We'll be able to prove quite a good deal of your story from the position of your wife and the furniture. (*He takes off his coat and puts it on the day bed*)

Tom Yes, I see.

Bert She attacked you?

Tom Yes.

Bert Violently?

Tom Oh yes. (*He sits on the sofa*)

Bert Was your wife ever violent before?

Tom Frequently. Her first husband left her because she so terrorized him.

Bert Is he still alive?

Tom If you can call it that. He lives in Hove.

Bert Have you any children?

Tom Two.

Bert How old?

Tom Eleven and nine.

Bert Where are they now?

Tom Boarding school.

Bert Still, they'll bear out your testimony.

Tom What testimony?

Bert You've just said to me that your wife was violent.

Tom But I wasn't testifying. I was telling you as an old friend. That's quite different.

Bert No, it isn't. I came here officially as a policeman.

Tom I didn't know that. You came in as an old friend.

Bert So your story isn't true?

Tom Of course it is. But I can't say any of that in court. My wife was a saint.

Bert Not violent?

Tom Good God, no!

Bert So she didn't attack you?

Tom Of course she did. Do you think I'd make up such a thing if it wasn't true?

Bert If she wasn't violent, why did she attack you?

Tom Because of extreme provocation. It was very wrong of me. I hope I get a very heavy sentence. You must make sure I do.

Bert How did you provoke her?

Tom By being right. What can possibly be more maddening, more provoking than that?

Bert Right about what?

Tom I proved to her conclusively that I loved her more than she loved me. Humiliated past endurance by being proved wrong, she flew at me screaming with rage and slapped my face.

Bert How many times?

Tom Once.

Bert You said repeatedly.

Tom It could have been twice. Or even three times. They were very gentle blows, however. Nevertheless they maddened me. I think I must have regarded it as an assault on my virility. I shook her viciously. It was quite uncalled for. I am entirely to blame. Will you arrest me now? (*He rises*)

Bert After you shook her, what happened?

Tom I flung her brutally to the ground. (*He mimes the action*) There's no doubt about it, I am a fiend. (*He sits on the sofa and mimes taking a brandy and cigar*)

Bert I thought you said you tripped.

Tom Flung brutally to the ground sounds better, don't you think?

Bert is silent. He wanders vaguely round, watching Tom

Bert Why is that lamp on the floor?

Tom It fell in the struggle.

Bert If you flung her brutally to the ground, how was she able to struggle?

Tom I'll work that one out later.

Bert No, you won't. You'll tell me now.

Tom Well—she could have risen, couldn't she? And gone for me again. Yes, that's it. That'll work beautifully. *Then* we struggled.

Bert And tripped.

Tom Very probably.

Bert It's just as well I know you. Not a word of this is true. Oh, you're not lying. You just don't know what the truth is. I remember when we got pissed once in Cyprus, your account of what happened the next day bore no relationship to the real facts. Now. We may not have seen each other for years, but we're old friends, aren't we?

Tom Yes. Do sit down, Bert.

Bert (*Sitting on top of the bean-bag*) The point is . . .

Tom You sit in the middle. Not on the top.

Bert The point is . . . (*He traps his hand under the bean-bag as he sits. He falls forward, recovers, and sits on the top*)

Tom Comfortable?

Bert Yes. (*He falls backwards and then clambers back and sits cross-legged on the top*) The point is, I am a policeman. So I can only help you so far. In a little while it'll be out of my hands and then you'll be on your own. Since I know you, I won't be on the case. Now I know you couldn't be brutal, if you tried. Whatever happened must have been an accident. Now I advise you first of all not to give evidence in court. With your imagination and contradictory stories, a prosecuting counsel will tie you up in knots. And secondly, the only way, the *only* way you'll survive is if you tell the truth.

Tom I have.

Bert No you haven't. But you're going to. I'm going to call the station in a moment and then you'll probably be taken there in a police car and you'll be questioned. Now just answer them "Yes" or "No". See? If you have to go into further detail, keep it brief. We'll have a little rehearsal. Did you have a row?

· *Tom mimes taking the oath*

Tom Yes.

Bert Did she lose her temper?

Tom Yes.

Bert And she then attacked you?

Tom Yes.

Bert She slapped you?

Tom Yes.

Bert Splendid. Did she slap you more than once?

Tom Oh yes. It was a savage assault.

Bert No, it wasn't.

Tom No, it wasn't.

Bert We'll pretend you didn't say that.

Tom I didn't. I'm sorry.

Bert Did she slap you?

Tom Yes.

Bert More than once?

Tom Yes.

Bert And then you tried to stop her?

Tom Of course. Don't you find this terribly dull?

Bert Dull or not, keep it brief. You struggled together?

Tom Yes.

Bert For roughly how long?

Tom Hours and hours. Exhausted we fell . . .

Bert For how long did you struggle?

Tom A couple of minutes.

Bert You tripped?

Tom I suppose so.

Bert And the fall killed her?

Tom I imagine so.

Bert Right. Now listen to this. My wife and I had a row. She lost her temper. I tried to control her. We struggled and fell. She was killed in the fall. I then called the police. Is that a true statement?

Tom If you say so. It sounds very unconvincing to me.

Bert It's a bloody sight better than your flights of fancy. What's your solicitor's number?

Tom His office will be closed.

Bert His private number.

Tom I don't know.

Bert This is an emergency. At all costs you must be stopped from talking. If you're not careful, you'll talk yourself to the gallows.

Tom Hanging's abolished.

Bert For the first time I see why. Even so I wouldn't put it past you to petition Parliament to reintroduce it specially for your case. You're a raving lunatic. You shouldn't be allowed out loose. What's his name? (*He rises and picks up the local directory*)

Tom Whose?

Bert Your solicitor.

Tom Smith.

Bert You're joking. Tell me you're joking.

Tom It's true. It's God's own very special truth. And what's more it's John Smith.

Bert Where does he live?

Tom London.

Bert What's his address?

Tom I don't know.

Bert All right. Who does your business affairs?

Tom I do.

Bert That's not possible.

Tom Well, I do as I'm told really.

Bert Who tells you?

Tom My agent.

Bert Where is he?

Tom Out.

Bert How do you know?

Tom I rang. His secretary said he was out. He leads a life exclusively devoted to pleasure. It's absolutely monstrous.

Bert When did you ring?

Tom Before.

Bert For Christ's sake! Before what?

Tom Before I rang you.

Bert And after . . . ?

Tom Yes.

Bert What time?

Tom Six. Six-thirty. How do I know?

Bert After office hours.

Tom Oh yes. He works night and day. He's in his office at nine, works right through to seven. Even during lunch hour he's slaving for his clients.

Bert Did you leave a message?

Tom Yes.

Bert Go on. Go on.

Tom I'm trying to be brief.

Bert You switch from one extreme to another like a demented yoyo.

Tom I asked him to call back or to drop in.

Bert Drop in?

Tom He lives nearby.

Bert Is he likely to?

Tom Drop in? Yes.

Bert Thank God. Can he control you?

Tom I'm putty in his hands. I always do exactly as he tells me to.

Bert Now I'm going to call the station, but before I do listen to me very very carefully. On no account answer any questions or make any statements without your solicitor being present.

A car draws up

Tom That'll be Bill. (*He rises and moves to the front door*)

Bert It could be the Inspector.

Tom Why? (*He goes to the large window and looks out*)
Bert He knew I was walking round. He was going to look in if I wasn't
  back soon.
Tom Oh God!
Bert What?
Tom It's my mother-in-law.
Bert That's not funny.
Tom No, it is not funny!
Bert It's not really her?
Tom It is. What do we do? You must help me. She's paying off her driver.
Bert All I can say is she's in for a shock.
Tom So she is. It'll kill her.
Bert Don't be silly.
Tom I'm not. She's very old and frail with a weak heart and it will kill
  her to see Annabel there.
Bert I'll stop her coming in.
Tom She'll wonder what's wrong. She'll get alarmed and frightened. We
  must tidy up.

Tom starts frantically tidying up the trolley.

Bert Stop that! You're destroying evidence.
Tom Never mind.
Bert But it's a crime.
Tom Annabel, we must hide Annabel!
Bert What?
Tom Shove her under the desk. Help me. (*He moves the chair away from
  the desk. He grabs Annabel and starts to lift her*)
Bert Don't touch her. Stop it, you bloody fool!
Tom Let go of me!
Bert I'm arresting you.
Tom Pompous ass!
Bert Don't you see what you're doing? The evidence in this room will
  help you. If you destroy it, you're destroying your defence.
Tom I refuse to frighten my mother-in-law to death. Get her legs.

Mrs Cartwright, off, calls "Hullo!"

Bert Oh God, why didn't I get on to the station at once?
Tom If we leave Annabel here, it will kill my mother-in-law and you will
  have murdered her.
Bert Why didn't you tell me she was coming?
Tom I forgot.
Mrs Cartwright (*off*) Annabel! Are you there?
Bert Don't answer that. She'll think you're out.
Tom With the lights all on? Besides, Annabel fixed it only this evening.
Bert Now you tell me.

The front doorbell rings impatiently

  O.K. Under the desk.

They hastily shove the body under the desk, head first

Tom Shove. Oh God! You can see her legs. (*He tries vainly to put her leg into the desk drawer, then covers her legs with scripts from the desk*)
Bert Right. Into the chest with her. (*He wheels out the chest from under the stairs*)
Tom Oh, I couldn't. Think of *Rope*. Oh what a marvellous play that was.
Bert (*opening it*) Oh Christ, the chest is full, stick to the rules, stick to the rules. (*He pushes the chest back under the stairs*)
Mrs Cartwright (*off*) Tom!
Bert Into the cupboard. (*He opens the lavatory door*)
Tom It's a loo.
Bert I don't care if it's a cesspit. In she bloody well goes.

They pick Annabel up and start to carry her. Mrs Cartwright knocks on the front door

Is it the only loo?
Tom No, no.

Tom drops Annabel's feet, and points upstairs. Bert drops her head and trips forward

Oh, sorry, Bert. It's upstairs, turn right.
Bert No, no. It's out of order, see? So she's got to go upstairs.

They pick Annabel up again and go to the lavatory door

Can you lock it?
Tom From inside with a bolt.

By now Annabel has been shoved in the lavatory. Mrs Cartwright knocks on the door

Bert Let her in.
Tom O.K.
Bert I'll tidy up. Keep her at the door as long as you can. (*He goes to the trolley and clears up the mess*)
Tom O.K.
Bert We've committed half a dozen serious crimes. You realise that. Talk about Watergate. I bloody hope your mother-in-law lives to be a hundred.

Tom goes to open the front door. Bert frantically tidies up the evidence of the fight

Tom I'm so sorry, love.
Mrs Cartwright I've been knocking on this door till my knuckles were bleeding. What kept you?
Tom A crisis.
Mrs Cartwright Well, let me in.
Tom Watch out!

As Mrs Cartwright tries to get in he grabs the hem of her coat and holds it up against the door frame

Mrs Cartwright What?
Tom Your coat is caught. On a nail.
Mrs Cartwright Oh.
Tom Stay still. We don't want to tear it.

Mrs Cartwright struggles out of her coat. Bert picks up the standard lamp and stands holding it

Mrs Cartwright I'm dying of exposure. I'd rather have this coat torn off me than suffer this cold any longer. (*She comes in firmly*) You were a time. (*She sees Bert standing awkwardly with the lamp*)
Tom Bert and I were doing some spring cleaning. I forgot to put something away and Bert and I were having hysterics. (*He shuts the front door and hands Mrs Cartwright's coat to Bert*)
Mrs Cartwright I'm quite exhausted with all that shouting. You must be deaf.
Tom So sorry, love. Do sit down.
Mrs Cartwright Yes, I will. (*She sits on the sofa*)
Tom This is an old friend of mine, Bert Hopkins. Bert Hopkins—my mother-in-law, Mrs Cartwright.
Mrs Cartwright How do you do.
Bert How do you do.
Tom Sit down, Bert. You must be dying for a drink.

Bert sits uncomfortably on the bean-bag, holding her fur coat

Mrs Cartwright Oh, I am!
Tom Your usual tipple? (*He goes to pour a Scotch*)
Mrs Cartwright Please. Tell me, Mr Hopkins, are you anything to do with the theatre?
Bert No. (*He jumps up, puts the coat on the day bed, then sits again on the bean-bag*)
Tom We met in the army.

Tom hands Mrs Cartwright her drink. Tom seems perfectly poised. Bert can hardly speak

Mrs Cartwright Oh, thank you.
Tom Bert?
Bert Whisky.
Tom Soda? (*He pours Bert's drink*)
Bert Neat.
Mrs Cartwright How's Annabel?
Tom Fine.
Mrs Cartwright I thought her looking a little peaky.
Tom She's not quite at her best, perhaps.
Mrs Cartwright Is she upstairs?
Tom I'm sure of it.
Mrs Cartwright Sure of what?
Tom That she's gone upstairs. I mean, she wouldn't be downstairs, would she?

Mrs Cartwright What are you talking about? You haven't got a cellar.

Tom I was joking.

Mrs Cartwright I saw your landlady, Mrs Stewart-Dubonnet, yesterday. She really is an intolerable old woman. Having a blazing row in a shop.

Tom Typical. Annabel ignores her. I'm afraid she so infuriates me I fight back. Bert! (*He turns Bert's head to face Mrs Cartwright and hands him his drink*) Have you come across her?

Bert Yes.

Mrs Cartwright Oh, you live locally.

Bert Surbiton. She's well known. Her hobby is fighting lawsuits. It's pathological.

Mrs Cartwright I should imagine so. So you and my son-in-law were in the forces together.

Tom National Service. I was the last man to be called up.

Bert They took one look at him and abolished conscription.

Tom Very good, Bert. (*To Mrs Cartwright*) Bert was my sergeant and spent most of his life shouting despairing orders at me . . . I was terrified of him.

Mrs Cartwright You always say you're terrified of everyone. Such nonsense.

Tom On the rare occasions when he wasn't shouting at me, he was keeping me out of trouble.

Bert How is this going to end?

Tom I created such chaos in the army I was known as Archbishop Makarios's secret weapon.

Bert He can't go on talking all evening.

Tom (*to Bert*) He'll have to. (*He turns to Mrs Cartwright*) There was a notice in the Barrack Room saying on no account can Private Bryce be allowed to touch anything.

Mrs Cartwright (*starting to laugh*) You're making that up.

Tom I'm not. (*He kneels by her side*)

Bert I mean when your wife never appears she's bound to notice eventually.

Tom We'll cross that bridge when we come to it.

Bert It'll blow up in our faces.

Mrs Cartwright Don't tell me you blew up bridges.

Tom Yes, we did. And we burnt boats, too.

Mrs Cartwright Good heavens.

Bert What do we do then? Answer me that.

Tom (*rising*) You wouldn't believe my incompetence. On one occasion I ruined months of peaceful negotiations.

Mrs Cartwright How?

Tom We were pacifying a village and I was in the loo.

Bert Oh God.

Tom Well I was . . . I was in this other loo, minding my own business when I was attacked by a wasp. (*He sits on the sofa*)

Mrs Cartwright starts to laugh

I assure you. This wasp made a direct and rather painful hit on a portion

of my anatomy not usually exposed to hazards, not even in the army.
Well, I screamed blue murder and rushed out into the street.

Bert Half naked.

Mrs Cartwright Good heavens.

Bert I couldn't stop him.

Tom You didn't try. You were screaming with laughter.

Bert And the balloon went up when he rushed up to a woman waved it
at her and asked her to sprinkle vinegar on it.

Tom For a wasp sting. I was in a blind panic. I thought it would drop off.
I was ready to lay down my arms, but I wasn't going to lay anything
else down.

*Mrs Cartwright laughs heartily. Tom and Bert join in over-enthusiastically.
Suddenly Mrs Cartwright stops laughing, collapses and dies*

Bert Christ.

Tom She's probably fainted.

Bert (*rising*) Water.

Tom (*rising*) Brandy's better.

Bert Lie her flat.

*They do so, and as Tom gets the brandy Bert feels her pulse, then closes her
eyes*

Tom What's the matter?

Bert She's dead.

Tom She can't be!

Bert She is. We've hidden your wife so as not to frighten your mother-in-
law to death and the silly bitch goes and dies on us anyway.

Tom I don't believe you.

Bert It's true. I've become a criminal for nothing. Fifteen years I've been
in the force, fifteen bleeding years, without a stain on my character.
People have tried to bribe me. Yes. And I refused them all. Hardened
criminals have tried to make me strike them and I've controlled myself.
Bloody demonstrators have insulted me, kicked my balls in, and still
I've kept control of myself. I am a blameless character. Until today.

Tom You're still blameless. It was I who made the mistake.

Bert Mistake. I'm ruined, that's what.

Tom No, no. (*He steps into Bert who backs away to the lavatory door*)

Bert You're a walking time-bomb. You're a danger to the public. Once
in Cyprus the whole bleeding army covered up for you when you nearly
killed Harold Macmillan. I intend to remove you. (*He takes off his tie*)

Tom Remove me?

Bert Murder you. (*He moves to the front door, pinning Tom against the
frame*)

Tom Now, Bert, keep calm.

Bert I'm a kindly man.

Tom Absolutely sweet. I've always said so.

Bert So if you don't struggle, I won't hurt you. It'll all be over in a
moment.

Tom Listen to me. You're in a state of shock. You haven't committed any crime at all. Certainly not a serious one.

Bert I don't want to hurt you, I really don't.

Tom My mother-in-law had a heart attack. You didn't kill her. And as for my wife, I killed her. I did it alone. I shall say so. I've been trying to say so all evening. The evidence. All right, we destroyed the evidence, but for an excellent and moral reason. If you go mad and murder me, then and only then will you really be criminal.

There is a pause. Bert puts on his tie again. Tom screams, thinking he is going to be strangled

Bert You're quite right, of course.

Tom Yes.

Bert It's O.K. I've recovered.

Tom Thank God. You frightened the life out of me. (*He pours himself a Scotch*)

Bert You won't die. You won't ever die. I realized that in the army. You're indestructible. Flapping round, screaming with agitation, swearing you're terrified, on you go, relentlessly, driving stronger and tougher men to premature graves . . .

Tom Never mind about all that. What are we going to do now?

Bert Call the station. (*He sits at the desk*)

Tom What do we tell them?

Bert The truth.

Tom Even I don't believe it.

Bert Nor do I. But we'll tell it, nevertheless.

Tom We can't say my mother-in-law died laughing. It's ludicrous.

Bert No more ludicrous than the reason for your row with your wife. But as that's the truth, that's what we'll tell. We must pray they believe us, because we can't prove anything any more. We can't prove where your wife fell. She could have fallen anywhere. We can't prove you fought with her. Or that she attacked you. Make no mistake about it, we're in one hell of a mess.

Tom We can prove my mother-in-law had a weak heart, and that explains why we hid Annabel.

Bert Do you benefit from their deaths?

Tom Oh yes.

Bert Christ! Every bloody thing's against us.

Tom What do you mean?

Bert You've a motive.

Tom For what?

Bert Murder.

Tom Murder?

Bert Look. Your wife is killed. You destroy all evidence how. Your mother-in-law comes in and dies of a heart attack, we know how and why, but no one else does. You could have let her see Annabel's body to frighten her to death. If we both thought that possible, so will others.

Tom You don't benefit.

Bert We're old friends. I insisted on answering your call.
Tom That proves my innocence.
Bert No, it doesn't. What if we planned it all? You knew what station I was in, when I was on duty.
Tom But I didn't.
Bert You could have done. I could have told you. We're sunk without trace.
Tom You can't be. You have no motive.
Bert I need money.
Tom Oh God!
Bert I'm in debt. Not badly, but in debt nevertheless. You're earning a good deal now. A good prosecutor could make mincemeat of us.

A car draws up

That saves us a telephone call. (*Rising*) It'll be the Inspector.
Tom I'm not going to allow this to happen. You haven't committed any crime at all. I have. So I alone must be punished. We'll put my mother-in-law in the loo too, then all you have to say is that my call was entirely frivolous. I thought I'd seen a burglar. You saw no evidence of anything and left.
Bert Why would you have hidden them.
Tom Panic.
Bert It'll make things worse for you.

The car reverses

Tom No, it won't, and it won't matter if it does. I killed my wife. I really did kill her. I should be punished.
Bert Why did I stay so long?
Tom Old times.
Bert You'll look so callous. What is he doing with that car?
Tom Driving away.
Bert No he isn't. He's having difficulty parking.
Tom We haven't a second to waste. Help me.
Bert Leave her.
Tom At least you won't be in trouble and only I will. I'll bloody well do it on my own. (*He puts Mrs Cartwright over his shoulder and carries her towards the lavatory*)

The front doorbell rings

Let him in while I shove the old dear in here. (*He opens the lavatory door*)

Annabel falls out

Oh Christ! Shove them in.
Bert (*doing so*) We'll go to jail for life.
Tom Nonsense.

Annabel falls out again

Bert She's fallen out again.

Tom She's dead, but she won't lie down.
Bert Heartless bastard. You've no feeling at all.
Tom When I'm dead you can feed me to the sharks for all I care.
Bill (*off*) Hullo! Anyone there?
Bert That's not the Inspector.
Tom It's Bill.
Bert Bill who?
Tom My agent.
Bert Tell him to go away.
Tom I can't. He's come specially.
Bert Oh God, oh Christ, oh Hell!
Tom What do I do?
Bert I don't know.
Bill (*off*) Hullo—Tom!
Tom Shove her back in again.

They push Annabel back into the lavatory

Bert That door will fly open again.
Tom Well, wedge them up against the cistern.

Bill knocks on the door

Bert Don't let him come in.
Tom How can I stop him? (*He struggles with Annabel's body*)
Bert Has he ever done you any harm?
Tom No.
Bert Then you've got to save the poor bastard from coming in. Tell him you've the plague. (*He throws Mrs Cartwright's coat into the lavatory*)
Tom He won't suspect anything. We must just brazen it out. He's driven miles to see me. (*He goes to the front door*)
Bert Mark my words, we'll get thirty years.

   Bert slams the lavatory door and leans against it, as Tom opens the front door

Tom Nonsense. Come in, Bill.
Bill I've had the most exhausting day. Pamela gave me your message. What's up?

Bill enters

Tom Nothing.
Bill Nothing?
Tom Nothing at all. Still, I'm delighted to see you. May I introduce you. Bert—Bill. Bill—Bert. (*pause*) Bert's just a little bit tired. Have a drink.

Bill and Bert nod briefly to each other

Bill Pam said you were hysterical.
Tom That's nonsense.
Bill She said you were out of control, were in a terrible state.
Tom You know how she exaggerates.

Bill I left Sir Peter arguing about his contract. I've not telephoned forty-two different people. My wife may well leave me because I'm late again and you tell me it was all a mistake.

Tom It was a very bad line. I thought she was having a fit, too.

Bill Well, you're upset about something. I can always tell.

Tom Whisky, gin, sherry, brandy.

Bill (*sitting on the sofa and putting his briefcase on the floor by him*) A large whisky. I've been driving for hours, I intend to make sure some of your ninety per cent is spent on me.

Tom pours Bill a huge whisky, full to the brim

Tom Soda?

Bill Please.

Tom pretends to add soda, making a "swooshing" noise

Tom Cheers.

Bill Cheers. Well, I didn't expect you to spend it all at once!

Tom Bert's an old friend of mine. Sit down, Bert.

Bill You a writer, too?

Bert No. (*He sits on the desk chair*)

Bill Very wise. Has he been in a state?

Bert A bit of one.

Bill There you are. What was wrong?

Bert He couldn't think what to do with a corpse.

Bill I knew it! It's getting more and more difficult to think of a fresh gimmick. Murder's easy. Tom's marvellous at murder. It's disposal of the bodies which is his difficulty. What was wrong?

Tom Let me tell you the plot. There's this couple. (*He sits on the sofa*)

Bill Yes.

Tom They have a row. Not about another man or woman, but how much they love each other. They lose their tempers and come to blows and she gets killed accidentally.

Bill Yes.

Tom Then the husband panics and rings up the police.

Bill As that's the most sensible thing to do, how has he panicked?

Tom Well, he has. I would. He would. Well, then the police send someone round and it's an old friend.

Bill He didn't know it would be?

Tom No.

Bill He's alone.

Tom Yes.

Bill He wouldn't be. There'd be two policemen. They work in pairs. They always do.

Tom There has to be only one.

Bill Isn't that contrived?

Tom No. Why was there only one?

Bert Station is short-staffed.

Tom There you are.

Bill O.K. but I'm not convinced.

Bert They didn't realize the seriousness of the call.

Bill I see.

Tom Anyway, the policeman comes round and sees the body. He's about to ring up the station when the wife's mother turns up.

Bill Jesus wept. Why must it be the wife's mother, for God's sake?

Tom She has a weak heart.

Bill Can't an aunt have a weak heart? Or a friend? Or a neighbour? Why her mother? Mothers-in-law went out with the Charleston.

Tom It has to be her mother. In my mind it's her mother. It wouldn't seem real to me if it was anyone else. Anyway, he's frightened she'll die if she sees her daughter dead on the floor, so he persuades his policeman chum to help hide his wife and they do this and the mother turns up and she drops down dead anyway.

There is a dreadful pause

You don't like it.

Bill Not as it stands.

Tom Why not?

Bill It's not real. It's full of holes. A policeman would have more sense. And if anyone was to go to court with a story like that, really in court . . .

Tom They'd never be believed.

Bill Never.

Bert What about the mother-in-law's heart attack?

Bill Absurd. Unbelievable.

Tom But what would you say if the husband leaves the wife lying there. He rings up the police, leaves a garbled message and before the police can get to him, the mother-in-law turns up and dies of shock. The husband now has two corpses to explain away. So *then* he panics, hides the bodies. The police turn up and the husband, still in a panic, lies and talks nonsense about a burglar.

Bill That's much better. (*He rises*)

Tom (*to Bert*) See?

Bert I don't know. I'm not sure.

Bill His panic sounds more reasonable. Two corpses are far more difficult to explain away than one. I'll just use your loo. (*He opens the lavatory door and closes it*) Oh sorry! (*He opens the door again. He stands still for a horrified moment, slams the door, then turns and shrieks at them*) There are two bodies in there.

Tom I know.

Bill We must call the police.

Bert I am the police.

Bill starts gibbering with rage and shock

Bill You're mad. You're both mad. How dare you do such a thing to me! I'll sue you.

Bert Keep calm.

Bill I am calm. You should see me when I'm in a state.

Bert I've been through all this. First of all incredulity. Then anger. Then shock. Then finally, stunned disbelief.

Bill Where are the rest of the police? Where's your lawyer? How dare you ring me up! You should both be certified. What the hell happened?

Tom I told you.

Bill What?

Bert The plot. The bad, contrived, unbelievable plot is what happened. The first plot.

Bill It can't be true.

Tom It is.

Bill Annabel. You killed Annabel? (*He sits on the bean-bag*)

Tom Yes.

Bill Why?

Tom I told you.

Bill You seemed so happy.

Tom We were happy. Don't look at me like that. You have rows with your wife.

Bill I haven't killed mine.

Tom That's only by a miracle. Every time you both step in a car, you turn on each other like tigers. I'm amazed you haven't ended up under a lorry.

Bill Be that as it may . . .

Tom All married couples have rows every day and contrive to be very happy indeed. I just got carried away.

Bill Carried away!

Tom I'm not minimising what I've done, but I did not do it with malice aforethought. Now I agree I should never have rung you, but I did it whilst petrified with panic, and when I came to my senses I hoped you would never be involved, but you are. So what do we do now?

Bill Tell the truth.

Tom I tried to, only Bert turned up.

Bert Then when her mother turned up, we hid Annabel.

Bill (*rising, and moving to the front door*) I will go to the local station and tell them. You two stay here. I'll return with a posse of police officers and we'll take it from there.

Bert He needs a solicitor.

Bill Yes.

Bert His is called Smith, so you'll never trace him.

Bill I'll get mine, poor sod.

Bert Whoever he is, he must stop Tom from talking. He made a statement to me which reduced me to tears. If he repeats it he'll get the full rap for murder.

Bill O.K. But I'm going to tell the police first.

The front doorbell rings

I'll answer it. (*He opens the door*)

A woman of late middle-age stands in the doorway. She stares arrogantly at Bill, blocking the way out

Mrs Stewart-Dubonnet My name is Mrs Stewart-Dubonnet. I own this house.

Bill Really.

Mrs Stewart-Dubonnet Is that your car?

Bill Very probably.

Mrs Stewart-Dubonnet Kindly remove it.

Bill I'm just going to.

Mrs Stewart-Dubonnet At once, do you hear? It's blocking my entrance.

Bill That's the last thing I'd want to do.

Tom (*rising*) It's all right, Bill. This is my landlady. Mrs Stewart-Dubonnet. She's always very rude to everyone on sight. So you mustn't mind if she's rude to you. She was very badly brought up.

Mrs Stewart-Dubonnet Get out of my house.

Tom I pay rent for it, so it's mine.

Mrs Stewart-Dubonnet I've been watching you. Cars driving up at all hours of the night. Strange men. I've a good mind to tell the police.

Tom That's an idiotic threat. You're already well known to every local police station as a public nuisance. I know for a fact you've been arrested twice. So you are in fact a petty criminal.

Mrs Stewart-Dubonnet I'll have you up for defamation.

Tom And I'll have you forcibly ejected.

Bill Now, Tom.

Tom (*to Bert*) You don't have to put up with her. I do. She lives opposite me, she's intolerable and she's fought everyone in the village.

Bert That's right.

Tom She sues everyone in sight. She runs through solicitors like shit through a goose. Normally you pick on people who are silent or run from you like startled rabbits, but this time, you horrid old hag, you've chosen the wrong person to fight with.

Tom lunges at Mrs Stewart-Dubonnet: Bill grabs him and pulls him away

Bill Be quiet, Tom. We have a crisis on our hands. Leave her alone.

Mrs Stewart-Dubonnet You owe me rent.

Tom That's a lie.

Mrs Stewart-Dubonnet Your cheque was insufficient.

Tom You refused to pay for the roof, which is your obligation. I deducted the builder's fee.

Mrs Stewart-Dubonnet I never agreed to his bill.

Tom You never do. To any bill. And why? Because you're a miser. The windows all stick. Last summer we nearly died of suffocation. You are trying to drive us out. Well, I won't go. Now or ever. I shall stay here, have the windows removed and then remade with rolled gold which you will pay for.

Mrs Stewart-Dubonnet Don't you shout at me.

Bill This is a ridiculous scene. (*He moves to the front door*) Will you let me pass?

Mrs Stewart-Dubonnet You've all been drinking. I know what goes on here. You're running a bordello. Where is your wife?

Bill and Tom look at Bert

Bert There aren't any women here.
Mrs Stewart-Dubonnet Ah ha! Homosexuals. I'll get on to my solicitor
first thing and have you thrown out.
Bill I want to get to my car.
Mrs Stewart-Dubonnet You're a socialist.
Bill What if I am? Just let me get to my car.
Mrs Stewart-Dubonnet I can smell a socialist a mile off. Robbing us all.
You talk about people's incomes. You never mention the tax we pay.
Do you? If I have twenty thousand pounds a year, I pay nineteen
thousand pounds a year in tax. What do you say to that?
Bill That you have wicked ancestors and incompetent accountants. But
I don't know or care anything at all about your financial affairs. All I
want to do is to get to my car.
Mrs Stewart-Dubonnet Do you own it?
Bill I must be deranged.
Mrs Stewart-Dubonnet Or is it on your expense account? A tax fiddle.
Bill All I want to do is to get to my car. Will somebody please tell me, is
that unreasonable of me?
Bert (*rising*) Now, Mrs Dubonnet . . .
Mrs Stewart-Dubonnet Stewart-Dubonnet. My husband's family was most
distinguished. His mother was a D'Arcy De Witt.
Bert If you would let my friend pass . . .
Mrs Stewart-Dubonnet I know all about that sort of friendship. I don't
care what anyone says, it shouldn't be allowed.
Bill You're a nasty evil-minded old woman and I've had enough of you.
I intend to get to my car if it's the last thing I do.
Mrs Stewart-Dubonnet You probably take drugs . . .
Bill Is there another way out?
Tom No.
Bill This house was designed by a madman.
Mrs Stewart-Dubonnet My husband designed it and he was a genius.
Bill He certainly wasn't an architect. Bert, can I use force?
Bert I wouldn't advise it. It's very easy to be provoked into a scene with
women like Mrs Stewart-Dubonnet. The thing is to stay silent until
they've exhausted all their venom.
Bill But we can't stand here for ever while she hurls insults at us. Am I
the only one who realizes our position? We face serious problems. I
must get past her.
Mrs Stewart-Dubonnet If you lay a finger on me I'll have you up for
assault.
Bert She will, too. It'll cost you years and years of trouble.
Bill Do you mean to say this Fascist hyena can stand there all night
screaming abuse at us and we have to sit and listen? I've never heard
anything so outrageous in all my life. Where's a window? (*He moves to
the large window by the door*)
Tom That one's stuck. None of the others open.

Bill None?

Tom None.

Bill What does she charge you for this Black Hole of Calcutta? Don't tell me. I don't want to know. One thing's certain. When you get to prison, which I expect will be very soon, you won't notice the difference.

Mrs Stewart-Dubonnet Prison! Did you say prison?

Bert That's torn it.

Mrs Stewart-Dubonnet You're all crooks. Or Communists. You're a collection of spies.

Bill I'm renowned the world over for my patience. I have now lost it. Together with my temper. I've had enough of the lot of you. Here we are with two dead women in the lavatory and all we do is stand and argue with this desiccated memsahib. (*As he speaks he opens and shuts the lavatory door*)

Mrs Stewart-Dubonnet *Two dead women!*

Bill In the lavatory. Yes. And what's more, one of them is his wife and the other is his mother-in-law—and the next time you choose to kill anyone, Tom, I should be very much obliged if you refrained from ringing me up and telling me about it.

Mrs Stewart-Dubonnet His *wife*?

Bill And his mother-in-law. And in case I've not made myself clear, I should be glad if you didn't ring me up again. Ever. You can find yourself another agent. There are limits and expecting me to cope with a loo full of corpses is going beyond them.

Mrs Stewart-Dubonnet (*suddenly screaming*) Help! MURDER! RAPE! HELP!

Bill Shut up. (*to Tom*) I'm getting on to my solicitor first thing and if he can't get me out of our contract before noon, I'll sack him and get one who can. Let me tell you, Tom, you are mad. Stark staring bonkers and I wouldn't be a bit surprised if this horrid old woman is your mother.

Mrs Stewart-Dubonnet Two dead women in the lavatory—two dead women in the lavatory . . . Help!

Bill Will you let me pass, you silly crow.

Mrs Stewart-Dubonnet Murderer! Rapist!

Bill pushes her aside furiously. Mrs Stewart-Dubonnet screams, hits her head against the wall and slides silently to the floor. Bill goes past her. The room is absolutely silent. Very slowly Bill returns

Bill Why is she silent?

Tom She's dead—I think.

Bill What?

Bert rises, feels Mrs Stewart-Dubonnet's pulse, then drops her arm

Bert Yes. Afraid so. (*He goes to the front door*)

Bill She can't be.

Tom But she is. Oh well!

Bill I—I brushed past her.

Bert You pushed her. (*He shuts the front door*) Violently.

Tom Don't worry, Bill. It'll only be manslaughter.

Bill Only!

Bert When you get used to the idea, it doesn't seem so dreadful. It takes an hour or two, but if they're spent, as mine have been, in this house, a few years in a peaceful prison seems quite attractive.

Bill A few years! Are you sure she's dead?

Bert Oh yes. I can tell at a glance now.

Bill I can't have killed her. I'm a pacifist.

Bert I might have guessed. Once a year all you pacifists try to kill me in Trafalgar Square.

Bill I'm a kindly man. I am really. I've been known to help old ladies across the road. Truly. I didn't know what I was doing. I've never been in such a rage in all my life. It was the shock of those bodies.

Bert Accidents will happen. (*He sits on the sofa*)

Tom Have a drink.

Bill sits on the sofa, picks up his glass, and drinks

Bill I must have gone mad! Did you go mad too?

Bert I guess so.

Bill Are you married?

Bert Yes.

Bill What will our wives do?

Bert I don't know.

Bill We'll go to jail.

Bert Yes.

Bill For ever.

Bert Well, for some time.

Bill It'll be terrible.

Bert Like the army. Only worse.

Bill I hated the army. I'm in far too much of a state to drive the car. We'd better ring the police.

Tom rises. He picks up the telephone, rattles the receiver, then puts it down

Tom You'll never believe me. But the phone's dead too. (*He makes the sign of the cross over the telephone*)

They all laugh hysterically

Bill Oh dear.

Bert We'll have to walk down to the station.

Tom And give ourselves up.

Bill For multiple murder.

Tom roars with laughter

Tom Their faces.

Bert Oh God, how funny. The poor bugger on duty is very, very slow and very, very stupid.

This sends them into transports of mirth

Tom It's terribly sad. It's our last free evening.
Bill I want another drink.
Tom You'll be drunk.
Bill I am already.
Bert Let's all get drunk.

Tom goes to the trolley, stepping over the body of Mrs Stewart-Dubonnet, picks up two glasses and a bottle, jumps over the body and sits on the sofa

Tom Long life!

They all have a drink. Tom starts to cry

Tom I loved Annabel. Really I did.
Bill Don't cry, Tom. I believe you. You were both—(*starting to cry too*)—both such a lovely couple.
Tom So were you.
Bert So were we. (*He starts to cry as well*) Oh God. It's awful. We're going to look such idiots in court.

Tom stops crying

Tom Well, come on. Let's go down. We must pull ourselves together. Look, you two, I've stopped crying.
Bill That's because you're so strong.
Bert Stronger than us.
Bill And braver too.
Bert Much braver.

Bill and Bert are sobbing uncontrollably

Tom There, there! It won't be as bad as all that. Really it won't. With remission we'll be out in—well, ten years—and who knows, we may all be put in the same cell. That'll be nice, won't it?

This is too much for Bill and Bert, who sob louder and louder as—

the CURTAIN *falls*

ACT II

The same. Half-an-hour later

They are all sitting in a state of complete despondency, Tom by the desk, Bill on the sofa, Bert on the bean-bag. Eventually Tom rises, sits, then speaks

Tom I have a plan.

Bill Oh God!

Tom No. Really. It's quite simple. Neither of you have to do anything. At all.

Bert I don't want to hear it.

Tom You both go away. Now. This minute. Bill drives Bert home and then goes home himself.

Bill Tom. I have killed an old woman.

Tom By accident.

Bill I got drunk and in a rage I stormed round the room like a tornado, then I shoved her aside so savagely that I nearly bashed her brains out.

Tom That's a gross exaggeration.

Bill No, it isn't. I lost complete control of myself. So I'm guilty of manslaughter and must, *must* go to jail.

Tom Why?

Bill Because . . .

Tom It was my fault. It all started with me. I must go to jail, not you.

Bert (*rising*) Poison! Do you have any poison in the house?

Tom No.

Bert (*sitting*) No, of course not. It was just a wild hope. And naturally you've no gun?

Tom Naturally.

Bert Never mind. I just thought it would be a good idea if we killed ourselves. You know. For a change. Instead of always killing defenceless women.

Bill That's what they'll say about us, won't they?

Bert Yes.

Bill They'll call us monsters.

Tom The monsters of Cosy Nook . . .

Bert That's right.

Bill We'd better go down now. Now we're more sober.

Bert I suppose so.

Bill You're a better judge of this than I am. What—what will we really get?

Bert I don't know. I just deal with respectable crimes like burglary and indecent exposure. Mass murder of old women's not in my line.

Tom Annabel wasn't old.

Bert Murders don't happen all that often on my beat, but roughly—Tom

killed Annabel and failed to report her death, as did Bill and I when we
found out. Then Tom and I tampered with the evidence of her death and
Bill has failed to report that too. Next, we haven't reported his mother-
in-law's death and we removed all evidence as to how that happened as
well. Tom and I have certainly conspired to defeat the course of justice
as has Bill now. After that, Bill killed Mrs Stewart-Dubonnet and none
of us have reported her death. So there you have it. Two deaths by
manslaughter, if not murder, conspiracy, one unexplained and im-
probable death. I reckon fifteen years.

Bill Each?

Bert Oh yes. Of course, as Tom benefits from his mother-in-law's death,
they may try to pin a murder charge on that too.

Bill Mother-in-law! God!

Tom If only you'd listen to me—just go.

Bert We can't do that.

Tom It's all so simple. I've worked it out and it's foolproof.

Bill Is it Tom proof?

Tom The time of death must be a bit obscured by now—so you called and
saw me *before* any of this happened. I called you up about some
imaginary burglar. We discovered we knew each other of old. I gave you
drinks. We chattered away about old times. That will explain why you
were here so long, Bert, and any fingerprints you left. Bill was never here
at all. I rang his office about a play I was in a state about. I often do—
and you decided to deal with it in the morning.

Bert Why wasn't he at home?

Tom Working late.

Bert His secretary?

Tom Pamela? Do you know when she left?

Bill Yes—no.

Bert Which?

Bill I rang when she was just leaving to see if there were any messages.

Tom That's how you knew about my call.

Bill Yes.

Bert What did you do?

Bill Swore horribly.

Tom So it's quite believable that you didn't come here.

Bill Quite. Where have I been?

Tom You went back to the office.

Bill What for?

Tom To get a script you had to read and had forgotten about.

Bill My wife would have rung me.

Tom You were only in the office for a couple of minutes. The rest of the
time you were driving back and forth. The traffic was appalling. It
always is. So Bill never came here this evening and Bert came before it
happened. What's wrong with that?

Bill First, you are charged with three deaths, not one, and I won't be
charged at all and nor will Bert.

Tom Nor will I. I can explain them all away.

Bill Good God. How?

Tom Annabel didn't die because I struck her since I never actually hit her at all. I shook her. That was all. I do believe if I'd kept my head when she died I wouldn't even have been charged. Panic started the chain of events. Panic. If Bert had taken me straight to the station or my mother-in-law hadn't turned up, all would have been well. Annabel died because she hit her head when we tripped over. We can't prove the struggle. Nor can the police. Very well, let's not tell them there was a struggle.

Bert How did she die?

Tom (*rising to act out his story*) She tripped over something, fell, hit her head and died. No one can prove I touched her. Before I could call the police, my mother-in-law came in and died of shock. I desperately tried to telephone, but by then my phone was out of order, when Mrs Stewart-Dubonnet appeared. She saw the bodies, had hysterics, I tried to pacify her, she rushed to the door, hit her head and died. It's a bit far-fetched, I admit, but no more than the reality.

Bert You benefit from their deaths.

Tom Yes, but I don't need the money. For the first time in my life I'm solvent. Any motive I have for murdering them is more apparent than real.

Bert After Stewart-what's-her-name died, why didn't you go then?

Tom State of shock and terror. Besides, once you've left I'll go straight away.

Bill You're not considering it?

Bert It could just work.

Bill Never.

Bert His mother-in-law had a weak heart. That can be proved. They can check up with her doctor. There's no conspiracy charge. It's his word against the world's. He was happily married. He doesn't need money.

Bill But you've hidden the bodies.

Tom We must get them out again.

Bert (*rising*) But why haven't I been home or back to the station?

Bill Get them out? Get what out?

Tom Simple.

Bill Get what out?

Tom You're walking, aren't you?

Bert Yes.

Bill Answer me. Get what out?

Tom The bodies. They're in the loo. You're walking home. You see someone acting suspiciously and being ever so conscientious you follow him. In any case, no one will question either of you. They'll have their suspect. Me. Now come on. Give me a hand.

Bill (*rising*) Tom! They're dead.

Tom Exactly.

Bill We can't move them.

Tom Why not? Undertakers do.

Bill You're not a delicate squeamish writer at all. You're as hard as nails and as tough as bullets, you don't care.

Tom (*moving to the lavatory door*) Mrs Stewart-Dubonnet can stay where she is, but we've got to get the other two out. (*He opens the door and drags out Mrs Cartwright*)

Bill I don't like any of this.

Bert It's our one chance. (*Moving to the front door*) Come on.

Bill We're breaking the law.

Bert laughs

But we are!

Bert She wouldn't see Annabel straight away. I didn't.

Tom No.

Bill The police will see the bodies have been moved.

Tom I moved them in a panic. I'm capable of anything in a panic.

Bert I saw the body from here.

Tom Right. Hold her for me.

Tom shoves his mother-in-law to Bill

Now I'm Mama-in-law. (*He acts out Mrs Cartwright's arrival*) I come in. I come over here. I cross over to greet me. I turn. I see the body and I fall. (*He falls below the sofa*)

Bert (*pointing*) So she'd be over there.

Tom Put her here, Bill.

They start to move the body

Bill It's not as easy as you think. This arm is in the way.

Mrs Cartwright's hand gets caught in the coffee-table and she drags it along. Tom picks up the table and a leg falls off. Bill drags the body below the sofa

Tom A leg has come off.

Bert (*jumping*) What! Put her head in there.

Bill alters the position of Mrs Cartwright's head

Tom Shouldn't it be the teeniest bit . . .

Bert Her legs look all wrong too.

Bill tries vainly to rearrange her legs

Tom Come on, Bill. One should be more under the other.

Bill They won't go.

Tom Her arm is wrong as well.

Bill Don't bully me. I don't often arrange corpses

Tom You should take a course at Forest Lawn.

Bill I've no plans to make a profession of this.

Bert Move her arm still higher, Bill.

Bill I'm going to be sick.

Tom This is no time to be squeamish.

Bill Look, she's your mother-in-law. Do her yourself.

Bert Stand her up again and just let her drop naturally.

Tom Leave it to me. It's quite obvious that arranging corpses is an art like arranging flowers. (*He motions the others out of the way and rearranges the body with one arm draped artistically over the sofa*) You either have the touch or you haven't. Now if I put her arm here—see! She looks lovely. Quite as if she'd dropped there naturally.

Bert Beautiful.

Tom Thank you Bert.

Bill I think I've gone mad. (*He sits on the bean-bag*)

Tom You can go off your rocker as soon as you like, but wait until you get home.

Bill You're not just hard and tough. You're brutal. You've no feelings at all.

Tom Look, you're a humanist. You believe we become dust. Now I believe we have souls and that their souls have departed to a better and happier place. Which ever of us is right doesn't matter. We are agreed that their bodies are empty shells. So why make a fuss about them?

Bill What now?

Tom We must arrange Annabel.

Bill Your wife.

Tom That's it. My wife. She isn't here any more. If she'd died naturally she'd be laid out by now, then be put in a box and cremated. That is to say she'd be shoved in an oven and burnt and you'd be here comforting me. So just think of that. I am striving to save you both from my act of stupid folly. The least you can do is give me a hand. (*He goes to the lavatory door and then stands still*)

Bert I'll do it.

Tom Yes.

Tom turns away as Annabel is dragged out

Bert Give us a hand, Bill.

Bill O.K. (*He rises*)

Bert I found her here.

Bill Right.

They put Annabel on the floor by the sofa

Bert Not too bad. I'll just straighten the legs a bit.

Bill The head looks a bit odd.

Bert is at Annabel's feet and Bill is adjusting her head with Tom looking on when the Inspector walks in

Inspector Good God!

There is an appalled silence. He sees the other corpses

Whatever are you doing, Sergeant?

Bert Well, sir . . .

Tom You must be the Inspector? We've been expecting you. It's quite all right. I can explain everything. The body these two gentlemen are looking at is my late wife. This one here is my late mother-in-law, and this is my late landlady, Mrs Stewart-Dubonnet. There has been a series

of accidents for which I accept full responsibility, and to prevent any
more happening tonight I ought to be locked up at once. Is your car
outside?

Inspector Down the road. There was nowhere to park nearby.

Tom Let's go to the station, shall we? I shall come quietly. (*He puts the
Inspector's hand on his own shoulder*)

Inspector Just a minute. Sergeant!

Tom The Sergeant has been simply splendid. He called here earlier at my
request about what I thought was a burglary, but which wasn't at all.
And it's too extraordinary, we discovered we knew each other years
ago. So we had a drink, or even two. Then he left—

Tom and Bert look at each other

—but left his notebook behind. It must have dropped out of his pocket,
so he came back to collect it. By the time he returned these three women
had inadvertently died.

Inspector May I ask how?

Tom It was a chapter of accidents.

Inspector Evidently.

Tom All of them my fault. My wife tripped on this rug. (*He points to it*)
You see how it turns up? Well, I've been meaning to do something about
it and never did. Well, she tripped on it today, banged her head, and died.

Inspector She fell backwards?

Tom She was running backwards.

Inspector Why?

Tom Working out a bit of plot for me.

Inspector Plot?

Tom I write plays and I wanted to see what would happen if a woman
backed quickly from a man and tripped.

Inspector And what happens?

Tom She falls backwards and dies. I shall never try that experiment again.
When I realised she was dead—

Inspector How did you?

Tom Her heart had stopped. She wasn't breathing.

Inspector You didn't call a doctor?

Tom I tried to, but I got a deaf, senile, retired locum.

Inspector Has he gone home?

Tom She.

Inspector Well, where is she, or have you killed her too?

Tom She never came and it wouldn't have made any difference if she had
come.

Inspector Because she was dead already?

Tom No, she wasn't dead. Just deaf, senile and retired. Deaf. (*He spells
out D-E-A-F in deaf-and-dumb language*)

Inspector Did you think of ringing the police?

Tom Of course I did. But before I could do so my mother-in-law walked in. Well, when she saw her daughter lying there dead, she dropped down dead herself.

Inspector Must be catching.

Tom She had a weak heart.

Inspector I see. Anyway, now you could ring the police.

Tom So you would think.

Inspector Why didn't you?

Tom My phone went out of order.

Inspector You are a Jonah.

Tom It simply goes on strike, after three calls, quite regularly. I complain about it not less than twice a week. Anyway, I had just decided to drive to the police when my landlady appeared. She saw the bodies, had hysterics, I tried to control her and in so doing accidentally knocked her head against the wall.

Inspector So she died, too.

Tom By now I was hysterical as well.

Inspector I'm not surprised.

Tom I was in a state of shock and terror (*he sits at the desk*) so I'm afraid I just sat here panic-stricken.

Inspector (*to Bill*) And who are you?

Bill Bill Carlisle.

Inspector What are you doing here?

Tom He's my literary agent.

Inspector I was asking him.

Bill I'm his agent.

Inspector Why are you here?

Tom He brought me a script.

Inspector I am questioning Mr Carlisle.

Tom I'm so sorry.

Inspector Where is it?

Tom What?

Inspector The script.

Tom Here. (*He picks up a script from the desk*)

Inspector You have a lot of scripts to hand.

Tom Yes.

Inspector Very convenient. For emergencies like this. Why did you bring it?

Bill I thought he should do more work on it.

Inspector What's wrong with it?

Bill The plot is rather weak in places.

Inspector Was the sergeant here when you arrived?

Tom Yes.

Inspector Are you the prompter?

Tom No.

Inspector What were you doing when I arrived?

Bert waits for Bill to answer, then Tom, then realizes he himself is being questioned

Bert Me?

Inspector Yes.

Bert Well . . .

Inspector Hadn't you worked that bit out yet?

Bert No yes! I was seeing where she'd tripped.

Inspector And you?

Bill I thought she'd moved, so I was seeing if she was really dead.

Inspector Quick thinking. Sergeant, what have you been doing for two hours?

Bert I was here for some time. Then I left and began walking home.

Inspector A good distance.

Bert I felt like a walk. Anyway I observed someone acting suspiciously and followed them.

Inspector Did he commit a crime?

Bert No.

Inspector Led you down a blind alley?

Bert Blind alley sir. That's it. Anyway, about then I discovered I'd left my notebook behind and came back here—for it.

Inspector Well I'm glad you didn't take up a life of crime. You'd have been very bad at it. This is all a tissue of lies, which you're making up on the spur of the moment. And what I want to know is why?

Bert Why what?

Inspector Why everything. Why did you come here at all? Why is Mr Carlisle here? I don't believe either of your stories.

Tom Are you suggesting we're a bunch of criminals planning mass murder?

Inspector No I'm not suggesting that. No bunch of criminals planning mass murder would leave the front door open.

Bert I forgot to shut it. (*He shuts the front door*)

Bill Let me explain.

Tom It was all my fault.

Bert Tom, You've done enough explaining. (*He moves to one side of the Inspector*)

Tom I can manage everything. The thing to remember, Inspector, is I am responsible.

Bill I killed Mrs Stewart-what's-it. (*He moves to the other side of the Inspector*)

Bert There was his wife lying there, sir.

Bill and Bert are now on either side of the Inspector, talking rapidly through each other

Bill He didn't kill her.

Bert Yes, he did.

Bill No. I did.

Bert Were you here earlier?

Bill Earlier than what?

Bert Before you were here.

Bill I can't be here earlier than I was.

Tom It's all perfectly simple . . .

Bill It's impossible to arrive somewhere before you do.

Bert Are you telling me it was you who killed her?

Bill You saw me.

Bert I wasn't here then.

Bill Yes, you were. I struck her.

Bert She didn't fall?

Tom You're getting in a muddle, Bill. You only pushed her.

Bert He pushed her?

Tom Well, don't you remember?

Bert I arrived later.

Bill You were already here.

Bert She was dead when I arrived.

Bill I had a row with her in front of you.

Bert Tom had a row with her.

Bill No, no, it was me. He had one first, of course. They fought each other on sight. Then she picked on me.

Bert That was the other woman.

Tom There is no other woman in my life.

Bert I didn't mean that.

Bill You saw them fighting.

Tom We never fought. Not even when we were in the car together.

Bill (*moving to Tom*) What the bloody hell has that got to do with anything? At least I haven't throttled my wife and then stuffed her—

Tom (*rising*) What a disgusting thing to say . . .

Bill —*down the loo.*

Tom I've known for years you had a nasty streak in you. Always wanting me to make my writing more commercial. Cheaper and dirtier, that's what you mean.

Bill That's not true.

Bert We are *not* discussing your literary careers. Answer me one thing. Have you been here before?

Bill Often, but I never will again.

Bert Were you here earlier this evening?

Bill Of course not.

Bert So you didn't fight with and kill his wife.

Bill I've only killed one woman this evening.

Tom I killed my own wife, thank you very much. I certainly would never allow anyone else to kill her.

Bert Right! that's cleared that up, sir.

Inspector I'm still a tiny bit confused.

Tom If you would just leave it all to me . . .

Bert Tom killed Annabel and Bill killed Mrs Stewart-Dubonnet.

Inspector Yes, of course. I draw to your attention, however, that there are three corpses.

Tom Oh, that's my mother-in-law.

Inspector That explains everything.

Tom Well, it does in a way. I mean, would I be likely to plan mass murder with my own mother-in-law present?

Inspector Somebody said something about the loo.

Tom That was Bert's idea. It was really brilliant of him. That loo is in a *maddening* place, isn't it? Short of being bang in the middle of the drawing-room, it couldn't be in a worse place. I've never been able to find a use for it before today.

Inspector Did you intend to leave them there indefinitely?

Tom No, no. We hid my wife's body there temporarily.

A car is heard arriving

Bill (*to Tom*) There's a car.

Bert Are you expecting anyone?

Tom No.

Bill Who can it be? (*He looks out of the little window*)

Tom I've no idea.

Bill If it's a woman, keep her out.

Inspector It could be a police car. (*He looks out of the large window*)

Bill Thank God.

There is a sound of gears crashing

Inspector No, I'm wrong. It is a woman!

There is a sound of one car hitting another

Tom That's Isabel.

Inspector How do you know?

Tom She's never parked a car successfully in thirty years of driving.

The car hits another car. Bill runs across to the large window

Bill That's my car she's bashing. Somebody stop her.

Inspector I think I'll take her licence away now.

Tom It would be lovely, she's my mother-in-law's companion and she's crazy.

Bill She's a bloody maniac.

Another crash

She's bashing my car. (*He runs to the front door*)

Tom Don't argue with her. She can become quite violent—

Bill stops

—and we don't want any more accidents.

Bill No. No. We don't.

There is a tremendous crash

Oh God! (*He runs back to the door*) What's she doing now? My car is brand new. (*He looks over Bert's shoulder*)

Bert Front mudguard badly scraped, right door wrenched off. You must have left it open—careless of you, sir.

Tom (*standing on the chair by the desk*) We'll have to put all the bodies in the loo. She'll go stark, staring, raving mad if she sees them.

Inspector We can't do that.

Tom She's always going into nursing homes and having breakdowns.

Bert Don't listen to him, sir. (*He trips over Mrs Stewart-Dubonnet's body and falls behind the sofa*)

Inspector I'll keep her out.

Tom She must know my mother-in-law is here still and will insist on coming in. If you keep her out, she'll get frightened.

Bert We can both keep her out, sir. (*He appears suddenly beside the Inspector*)

Tom These women are dead. She's alive. We must think about her.

There is another loud crash

Bill She's hit a wall.

Tom She's already in a state. She's not as bad as this as a rule. She usually misses walls.

Bert If you listen to him we're sunk—

Bill Bert!

Bert —never mind about your car, you'll collect the insurance in jail—sir, I listened to him.

Tom We did the right thing.

Bert And that started the chain of events.

Tom It went wrong, but we were right to try.

Bert His mother-in-law died anyway.

Tom We didn't know she was going to.

Bert The evidence . . .

Tom It's destroyed already.

Inspector That's true.

Bert You'll be compounding a felony.

Tom If you let her in with those bodies lying all over the place you'll send a simple-minded woman into permanent lunacy. You cannot do it and I won't allow it. We are innocent of any intentional crime and you know we are.

Bill No woman can come in here. If she does, we'll kill her, we always do.

Tom The thing in any argument is to go to the heart of the matter and ask yourself what is the moral thing to do? Have you asked yourself that?

Bill We must learn from experience.

Bert And experience has taught us not to listen to Tom.

Isabel (*off*) Tom!

Bill Keep her out.

Inspector How?

Tom Hide the bodies.

Isabel (*off*) Are you there? Tom!

Tom We can't let her go mad. If she does I'll accuse you all in court. We don't matter. The dead don't matter. That poor fool out there does.

Isabel (*off*) Can I come in?

Tom (*calling out*) Isabel! What a surprise. Just coming.

Isabel (*off*) I drove into your wall.

Tom (*calling*) Oh! Fancy! With you in a second. (*He jumps off the chair*) (*To the others*) The shock of seeing all this could turn her into a mindless vegetable and it'll be your fault, Inspector.
Inspector He's right.
Bert He ought to be, but he isn't. Experience has taught us.
Inspector Come on, Bert. Help me. Keep her talking.

Tom goes to the door. We hear him talking off

Tom (*off*) Three cars including your own and a wall knocked down! You have excelled yourself, Isabel.
Isabel (*off*) I got in a muddle.
Tom (*off*) Let's have a look at the damage.

Bill hovers by the front door. The Inspector takes Annabel's head and Bert her feet. They push her into the lavatory

Bert Two were difficult enough. Three's going to be impossible.
Inspector We must just squash 'em in.

Bert and the Inspector put Mrs. Cartwright into the lavatory

Isabel (*off*) Is Elizabeth here?
Tom (*off*) Good gracious me, no.
Inspector Put the old woman sideways and then this one on top.
Bill (*wandering about*) He succeeds every time.
Tom (*off*) Don't worry about Mrs Stewart-Dubonnet's car. She won't be needing it any more.
Bert It'll be like the Black Hole of Calcutta.

Bert and the Inspector try without success to lift Mrs Stewart-Dubonnet, then drag her by her legs and heave her into the lavatory

Inspector Well, they aren't breathing, so that's all right
Isabel (*off*) It's all right. I'm fully insured.
Tom (*off*) Who did you get to insure you?
Bert Right. Standing room only.
Bill An evil genius, that's it.
Isabel (*off*) At least I haven't killed anybody . . .
Inspector We can always get a job in a mortuary.
Bert Or a sardine factory.
Inspector I can't shut the door.
Bert If we push together—one, two, three. That's it. (*They shut the door*)
Inspector Lock it.
Bert I can't. It only locks from the inside.

Isabel comes in with Tom as Bert and the Inspector are shutting the door. She stops. They stare at her as if she was a dangerous explosive

Isabel Oh.

Isabel walks into the room. The three men back from her. She holds out her hand and Bert goes to shake it but stops when Bill shouts

How do you do.

Bert How do . . .

Bill STOP!

Bert What?

Bill Don't touch her, Bert. She'll go to the loo if you touch her.

Bert Oh, yes.

Isabel It's quite all right. I don't want to go to the loo at all.

Bill Nobody does in this house.

Tom These are friends of mine. Bert, Bill and—and—oh, Ebenezer Entwistle.

Inspector How do you do.

Bill STOP! Remember what happened to the others. *In the loo.* We don't want anyone else to go to the loo ever. Do we? We don't like loos.

Tom What's the matter with you?

Bill I'm fine. I'm a man, so I'm all right. It's women who go to the loo in this house. Not men. Women always go to the loo.

Isabel I don't. I'm a fairy.

The men are silent

Are you all fairies too?

Bert It wouldn't surprise me if I turned into one after tonight!

Isabel It was an expression my mother used for people who never spent pennies. Miser was another! (*She turns to Tom, who backs away*) But it's too odd if Elizabeth isn't here, Tom. She left a note on the kitchen table saying Annabel rang her up and asked her to supper.

Tom Yes, she did. But they went out to eat.

Isabel Oh, I see.

Tom We were working.

They all mime working

Isabel Yes, of course.

Tom So she's not here.

Isabel I expected her home by now. She knows I don't like to be left alone at night. I get frightened.

Tom She may be back already.

Isabel Could I ring up?

Tom The phone's not working.

Isabel Oh, that explains it. I tried to ring you and couldn't get through.

Tom We've more work to do, so you'd better go home. Is your car all right?

Isabel I expect so. It usually is when I've run into cars before. I find it's better to do the hitting rather than to be hit.

Inspector You often have difficulty parking?

Isabel I used to. Now there are lots of lovely parking places, I don't any more.

Bert Most motorists find there are fewer parking places.

Isabel I know, I can't think why. The thing to do is to go where it says "at any time". You know, where the double yellow lines are. Good-bye, it's so nice meeting you.

Isabel exits, followed by Tom, who closes the front door

Bill She's never caught. That moving accident black spot drives like a tank and parks on blind corners and she's never caught. I have only to turn out on my drive to get a ticket. We have the world's most incompetent police.

Bert Never mind about that. She's escaped.

Bill That woman could drive blindfold up the M-one backwards in a fog and still escape.

The lavatory door burst open and the bodies fall out

Inspector Good Heavens!

Isabel comes in, followed by Tom

Isabel I think my car is too badly damaged . . . (*She sees the bodies*)

Bert rises. Isabel runs to the Inspector, who hides under the stairs

Bill Oh Christ!

Isabel starts to scream wildly

Inspector ⎫ Why didn't you keep her out? ⎫
Tom ⎬ I couldn't stop her. ⎬ (*Speaking together*)
Bert ⎭ It's all right, madam. ⎭

Isabel turns to Bert, who grabs the bean-bag and dives under the desk, barricading himself in

Bill I haven't touched her.

Isabel follows Bill, who jumps on the pouffe. She turns to Tom, who runs upstairs

Tom Isabel! I can explain everything.

Bill Don't touch her! Don't touch her!

Isabel turns and rushes towards Bill, grabbing his legs. They roll on the floor. Bill struggles to escape

Save me! I'll kill her. I'll kill her. Get her off me. I'll kill her if you don't.

Tom (*running below the sofa*) Isabel! Isabel! Fairies don't behave like this.

Isabel turns on Tom

Bill Don't touch her. She'll go to the loo if you touch her.

Bill runs and picks up the desk chair, holding it in front of him like a lion-tamer. He runs to the window, puts the chair down at the foot of the stairs, then runs up to the landing

Tom Don't fight. It's all right. I won't hurt you. (*He grabs hold of Isabel*)

They struggle together. Isabel picks up the arm of the sofa and hits Tom with it again and again, twirling him round like a top

I don't want to hurt you.

Bill Stop him! He'll kill her.

Bill runs down. Everybody shouts at once. Bert goes to help Tom. They fall on the sofa, leap up, and run upstairs. The arm of the sofa falls downstage. Bill runs upstairs, Isabel follows. Bill and Tom go through the door from the landing. Bert goes through the arch. Isabel goes through the door. Bert comes out from the arch, followed by Bill, Tom and Isabel. They all go through the door again except Isabel—Tom slams the door in her face. She turns, and sees Bert coming through the arch again. He dives through the banisters on to the daybed to escape her. Tom comes out of the door to the landing, followed by Bill. Tom runs downstairs and sits by Bert on the divan. Isabel runs downstairs. As she reaches the bottom the Inspector steps out and grabs her. He hits her with his fist and she falls on the sofa and rolls on to the floor below it.

Inspector (*triumphantly to the other men*) You see! (*Looking at Isabel*) Oh Christ!

Bill (*from the landing, calmly*) You've killed her.

Inspector Nonsense. I know what I'm doing. I merely knocked her out. I had to. She'd have done herself a serious damage if I hadn't.

Bill She's dead. It's inevitable. Women die as soon as they enter the house. We just have to accept that fact.

Tom and Bert rise

Inspector Don't be ridiculous.

Bill One, two, *three* and now four. Do we have to reach double figures before you realize that these deaths are not isolated events, but instead clear evidence of a malignant fate pursuing us remorselessly? Oh, it's not your fault, Inspector. Nor was it mine. If you hadn't killed her, fate would have removed her in some other way. You were merely the instrument. The innocent instrument.

They all look at Isabel horrified. She does not move. Bert picks up the arm of the sofa from the floor

Bert (*lifting her head with the tip of his shoe*) Yes. (*He goes to the window by the front door and puts the sofa arm on the floor*)

Inspector You saw me. Didn't you? You all saw me. She was running amok. It was an accident. We're taught how to deal with hysterics. She'd have hurt herself. I can't have killed her.

Bill But you have. We have all killed a woman this evening.

Bert I actually haven't. I've aided and abetted and destroyed evidence, but that's all.

Bill Well you'd better watch out or your turn may come.

Bert slams the front door

Inspector I've never hurt anyone. Never.

Bill Neither have I.

Bert Nor I.

Tom I haven't either.

The three of them look at Tom

    I know it's all my fault.

Inspector That's it! It's your fault. I had a blameless career, do you realize
that? I'm three years off from retirement and my pension, do you know
that? Now the least I can hope for is to be sacked with disgrace.

Tom Oh, I'm sure it won't come to that. Now listen to me . . .

Inspector I listened to you before and I never will again. I was going to
march you down to the station or at least keep that poor woman out
of here, but you talked me out of it. You are a danger to the community.

Bert That's right.

Inspector We wouldn't be here but for you.

Tom You didn't shut the loo door properly. Is that my fault?

Bert He's plausible, sir. You have to watch him.

Inspector You have ruined three men's lives—in one evening.

The Inspector takes off his tie: Bert does the same

If we go to jail for killing anyone, it will be for killing you.

Bert I nearly did him in earlier.

Inspector You should have done.

Tom What you are proposing to do to me is immoral. If you go to court
now you have a moral argument. (*He grabs the bean-bag and runs to the
trolley, holding the bean-bag as protection*)

Bert We have now. We are saving other men from you. I remember you
of old. You nearly caused the end of the world in Cyprus.

Tom How was I to know we were guarding a secret atomic station?
Nobody told me not to smoke. Bill! They're planning my murder. I
know they are. You must stop them. I will go now to the police station
and make a full confession and state categorically that I was responsible
for every death. I'll state that none of you had anything to do with any
of them. I've tried to do this all evening. The trouble is, you won't . . .

Bill The trouble is you talk too much. That's the only thing that's wrong
with you. So we must stop you, see?

Tom But, Bill, I can explain—

Bill Shut up. (*Slowly, taking off his tie*) Try being silent for at least five
hours or so. We've no need to kill him to stop him talking. Just tie him
up and gag him. The three of us are normal, reasonable, charitable men,
so we can't kill him. That would be wrong.

Tom, relieved, puts down the bean-bag

But we must silence him, and we must never listen to him again. (*He
suddenly leaps on Tom, pushing him down on the bean-bag*)

Tom screams

I've got him.

Bert Hold him.

Bill There is a rope in my car. In the boot.

Bert drops his tie and rushes out

Tom Let me go! Bill, you're crazy.

Bill We can quite easily kill you, so don't struggle.

Tom You're all mad. It's my fault. Inspector, you don't know what . . . *Don't do it!*

The Inspector runs and pins Tom's head between his knees; he uses his tie as a gag. Tom kicks wildly

Bill Hold his legs.
Inspector I've got them.

Tom breaks free, runs round the sofa to the front door

Bert enters with a rope. He drops it by the door

Bert No you don't.

Tom runs round the sofa again. Bert leaps across the sofa, tackles Tom, and they fall. Bill runs to the bottom of the stairs and brings down the chair

I've got the bastard.
Inspector Tie him up.
Bill Tie him to this chair.

The Inspector picks up the rope. Bill puts the chair by the desk. Bert puts Tom on the chair and ties him to it. Bill uses his tie to tie Tom's leg to the chair. The Inspector picks up Bert's tie and uses it to tie Tom's other leg. They all look at Tom triumphantly

Bert We don't want to kill him. Can he breathe?
Bill I don't much care if he can't. But of course he can breathe. If he'd been a woman we'd have killed him by now, but as he's a man he's still alive. And this is the crux of the matter. Women must be protected from us at all costs. We must keep women out of here.
Bert Yes.
Inspector How?
Bill Bolt and lock the front door.
Inspector Of course. (*He does so*)
Bert The windows stick. (*He checks the catch on the window*)
Bill They might break the glass and get in that way. We attract women like magnets and then they run into our fists, don't they? We must barricade them out. Help me move this bookcase.

Bert and Bill push a bookcase in front of the large window

Bert That's safe.
Bill (*moving to the chest under the stairs*) Help me with this chest.

Annabel, who is lying in full view of the audience, moves. Only Bill sees this —apart from the audience. He stands still, staring at Annabel in terror

Bert That's safe.
Inspector I'm not sure. Bill's right. Hundreds of women bent on self-destruction may charge the door like lemmings. We must put something against that too. Get a move on, Bill.

Bert puts the coffee-table on the sofa and lifts one end. The Inspector lifts the other end: they barricade the front door

Bert There.

Annabel moves again. Bill shrieks. Bert leaps on the sofa

What's the matter?

Bill She moved.

Inspector What?

Bill She moved. I tell you she moved.

Bert Who moved?

Bill Annabel moved. She moved, I tell you. I know she did. Twice.

Tom, who has been squeaking and struggling without ceasing, stops. There is total silence. All the men, hardly daring to breathe, stare at Annabel. Nothing happens

Inspector (*to Bert, quietly*) He's lost his reason.

Bert (*to Bill, soothingly*) It's all right, Bill. Just relax. We all get hallucinations sometimes, don't we? When you're in jail you'll get proper medical treatment and . . .

Bill There was that woman.

Bert What woman?

Bill In hospital. Dead. Certified dead. By doctors and nurses and everyone. I read all about it in the newspapers. For hours she lay there in bed in hospital dead. In the morgue—in the morgue—they realized she wasn't. She was about to be put in her coffin, shoved into the incinerator, when she sat up and asked for a cup of tea.

Tom struggles and squeaks furiously. The other three stare at Annabel. She does not move

Inspector Muscular reaction.

Bert Often happens.

Inspector Chickens do it every day when their necks have been wrung. Let's get the chest.

Bert and the Inspector turn to the chest. Annabel moves again and groans. Tom squeaks and struggles

Bill What was that?

Bert Tom.

Bill No.

Bert Yes.

Inspector He's never stopped squeaking.

Bert Did you groan?

Tom shakes his head

Bill It was her. I know it was. (*He rushes to Annabel*) Annabel! Annabel! Annabel! It's me. Bill. Your husband's agent. His best friend.

Tom (*muffled*) you bloody liar.

Bill Annabel! (*He lifts her half up and shakes her*) I only take a tiny percentage of his money. Wake up!

Nothing happens

Inspector It's useless, Bill. She's dead. They're all dead. Bert wouldn't make a mistake.

Bill What about those doctors? They did—in hospital, too. We must do something.

Annabel Oh.

Bill There. Somebody said "Oh".

Tom squeaks frantically

Shut up, you stupid bugger. Somebody said "Oh".

There is a pause

Annabel Oh.

Bill She's alive. She's alive. She's alive.

Inspector Did you look at her eyes?

Bert Of course.

Inspector Feel her pulse?

Bert Naturally.

Bill He made a mistake. That's all.

Inspector A mistake! (*He pushes Bert*) I'll have you demoted. (*He pushes Bert again*) I'll have you sacked. (*He pushes Bert again*)

Bert Did you examine any of them?

Bill She's alive, alive, alive.

Annabel Oh.

Bill Say it again and again and again.

Annabel Oh.

Bill You're alive. Women don't die as soon as they see us.

Annabel Well, of course I'm alive. (*She sits up, looks at the Inspector, then at Tom, then at the Inspector*) Oh. (*She subsides back to the floor*)

Bill She's died again.

Bert (*going to Annabel*) No, no, she fainted.

Inspector Bring her round.

Bert and the Inspector turn Annabel's body round

Bert Water. Water. Quick. Lift her, legs sir.

Bill runs into the kitchen. There is a loud crash. Bert follows Bill. They reappear, Bert carrying a large jug of water

Bert splashes a few drops of water on Annabel, with no effect, then up-ends the jug. Annabel shrieks and leaps up. Bill dances round, shouting. The Inspector begins taking off Tom's gag

Bill The jinx is broke. We don't kill women. We don't kill women.

Bert goes to Tom and helps to untie him. It looks as if he is hitting him with Bert pulling at a knot and Tom squealing and struggling to get free. Annabel grabs Bert

Bert Just lie still, you silly bastard.

Annabel Don't you hit my husband.

Bill It's all right. It's all right. It's all all right.

Pandemonium breaks out, everyone shouting at once

Bert	Jesus! He said you were violent. Help!	
Bill	Stop, Annabel, stop.	*(Speaking*
Annabel	Don't you dare murder my husband.	*together)*
Tom	Help! Help! I'm still tied up.	

The Inspector bellows at the top of his voice in the voice which has quelled a hundred riots

Inspector Quiet. SHUT UP! I am a Police Inspector and I will have calm. I AM A POLICE OFFICER, MADAM. KINDLY SHUT UP!

Annabel lets go of Bert, who falls to the ground then jumps up. There is total silence.

If you are still alive, Madam, the others could be too.
Annabel What others?
Tom Your mother, darling, and . . .
Bert (*pointing to Mrs Cartwright*) I'm afraid she had a heart attack.

Annabel screams, rushes to Mrs Cartwright and kneels by her side, rubbing her hand

Tom And died again.
Bert Again. What do you mean again?
Tom She went blue on an operating table once and for an hour or so they thought she'd died, but she hadn't. Then there was another time when she . . .
Bert Another time, what other time?
Tom At a wedding reception she . . .
Annabel Which one of you is the doctor?
Tom There isn't one.
Annabel What?
Inspector Artificial respiration. Quick!

Bert and Bill pull Mrs Cartwright into position: the Inspector pulls her head round, pointing downstage. They all do artificial respiration. Bert and the Inspector do mouth-to-mouth. Bill rolls Mrs Cartwright over and does it all wrong

Bill Face down. Work on the back.
Annabel Do you mean to tell me that you thought I'd died and you didn't even call a doctor! You not only don't love me more. You do not love me at all.
Inspector Get hot and cold water.
Tom Annabel, will you untie me.

Annabel exits to the kitchen.

Someone untie me.

Knocks are heard on the front door

Annabel enters with a bucket and pours water over Bert and Isabel

I can't do anything unless you untie me.

Annabel (*to Tom*) Our marriage has come to an end. You realize that, don't you.

Dr Sarah Hedley (*off*) Mr Bryce?

Annabel Any other husband in the world would have called a doctor.

Tom I did.

Annabel I knew that marriage to you was like dicing with death.

Sarah (*off*) Does Mr Bryce live here?

Annabel I didn't realize you were a homicidal maniac.

Annabel throws down the bucket and exits to the kitchen

Tom I did call a doctor. Is it my fault she was old and deaf?

Inspector Don't just sit there. Help your wife.

Tom I'm tied up. I'm tied up, you stupid Taffy bastard. I am tied up.

Annabel enters with two buckets of water

Annabel When I married you . . .

Bert takes one bucket and starts slapping Isabel with a wet curtain. Annabel throws water over the Inspector

Tom Tricked me into marriage . . .

Annabel You were starving in the gutter. I was loyal to you then, and I shall be loyal to you now.

Tom Loyal? About what?

Annabel About when you go to jail for mass murder.

Tom But I won't go to jail. I haven't killed anyone any more.

Bert stops to listen

Annabel I shall visit you in jail every day.

Tom Will you listen to me? The others will go to jail, not me. I'm in the clear now.

Inspector (*standing*) We want the water to put their extremities in, you silly woman.

Annabel Extremities?

Inspector Feet . . .

Annabel Feet!

Annabel rushes into the kitchen with her bucket

Sarah (*off*) Will you let me in?

Bert Oh God!

Sarah (*off*) I am a doctor. Dr Sarah Hedley.

Bert There's a woman out there.

Bill Keep her out at all costs

Bert throws the bean-bag at the door and hurls himself on top of it

Sarah (*off*) What's going on in there?

Inspector I am a Police Inspector. Piss off!

Annabel rushes in with another bucket of water and throws it over Bill

Tom If you had only acknowledged the fact that I love you more, none of
this would have happened . . .
Annabel You do not love me more . . .

On their continuing argument—

the CURTAIN *falls*

FURNITURE AND PROPERTY LIST

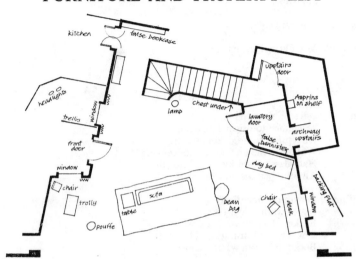

ACT I

On stage: Sofa, with detachable cushion arms
Bean-bag
Pouffe
Day bed. *On it:* cushions
Small chair. *On it:* drinks box with bottles of whisky, brandy, sherry,
  2 sherry glasses, 4 unbreakable whisky tumblers
Desk chair. *On it:* cushion
Desk. *On it:* telephone, message pad, writing materials, typewriter
  with paper inserted, scripts, desk lamp, show business photographs,
  oddments as dressing. On window-sill, local telephone directory,
  set of London directories, books
Coffee-table with detachable leg
Trolley. *On it:* cloth, cocktail-shaker, tongs, ice cubes, bottle of gin,
  bottle of tonic, empty sherry, brandy and martini bottles—all
  covered with cling-film, various empty small bottles, corkscrew,
  opener, etc.
Chest with false bottom. *In it:* 2 blankets at top to make it appear full
2 bookcases—one fake, the other with various books
Standard lamp, not practical, with bulb covered with cling-film
On shelf on stairs: bottle of aspirin

On stage: *On walls:* various pictures
            On front door: bolts. *On outside:* knocker
            False section in banisters
            Window curtains—one easily removable
            Carpet
            Rug
            Staircapet

Off stage: Briefcase **(Bill)**

Personal: **Mrs Cartwright:** handbag

ACT II

Set: **Bill's** briefcase on desk
            Telephone to original position
            Directories to original positions
            Whisky bottle on floor by coffee-table
            Half-glass of whisky by sofa for **Bill**
            All other glasses on trolley

Off stage: Length of rope **(Bert)**
            Jug of warm water **(Bert)**
            Bucket of warm water **(Annabel)**
            2 buckets of warm water **(Annabel)**
            Bucket of warm water **(Annabel)**

LIGHTING PLOT

Property fittings required: desk lamp, pendants, standard lamp (not practical, bulb covered with cling-film)
Interior. A living-room. The same scene throughout

ACT I, SCENE 1   Early evening

To open: All fittings (except standard lamp) on. Dusk outside windows

Cue 1   Tom: "I don't know what to do." (3rd time)   (Page 6)
            Fade to Black-out

ACT I, SCENE 2   A few minutes later

To open: As opening of Scene 1
No cues

ACT II, Scene 2   Half-an-hour later

To open: As close of previous scene

Cue 2   Tom: ". . . body there temporarily."   (Page 38)
            *Car headlights cross window: crossing again to coincide with
               various crashes*

Cue 3   Tom: ". . . think about her."   (Page 39)
            Loud crash—headlights off

EFFECTS PLOT

ACT I

ACT II